Railroad Yard

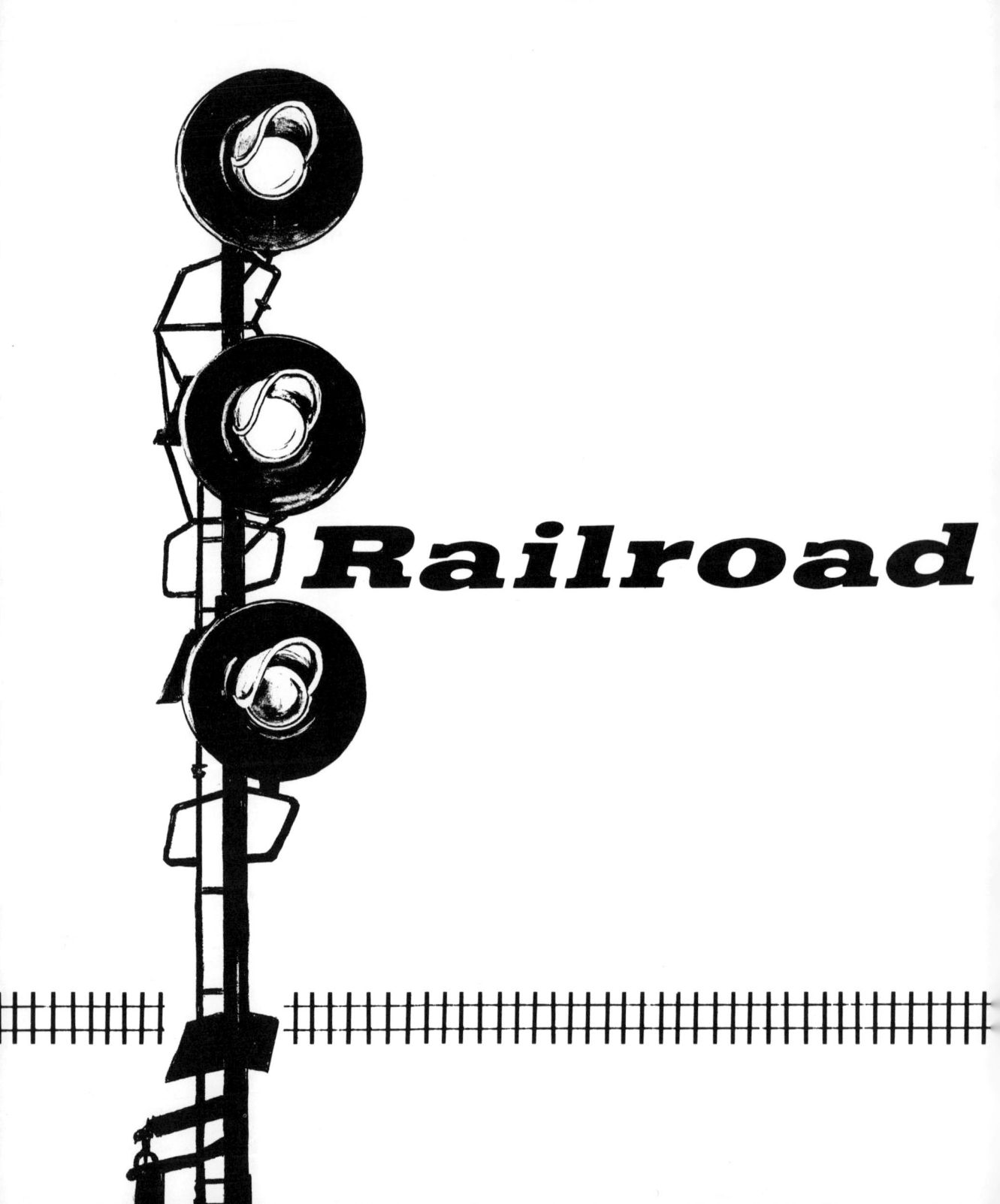

Yard

by Paul C. Ditzel

Illustrated with Photographs

Julian Messner New York

Copyright © 1977 by Paul C. Ditzel
All rights reserved including the right of reproduction
in whole or in part in any form. Published by Julian Messner
A Simon & Schuster Division of Gulf & Western Corporation
Simon & Schuster Building, 1230 Avenue of the Americas
New York, New York 10020

Printed in the United States of America.

Designed by Alex D'Amato

PHOTO CREDITS

Association of American Railroads, p. 8, 15, 39, 40
Mike Meadows, cover, p. 19, 20, 21, 22, 23, 25, 26, 27, 28, 29,
    30, 31, 32, 33, 34, 36, 37, 38, 43, 44, 45, 46, 47, 52, 54,
    56, 58, 59
Gary O'Malley, p. 40
Norfolk & Western Railway, p. 9
Santa Fe Railway, p. 13 (top), 14
Southern Pacific Transportation Company, title page, p. 11,
    16-17, 18, 42, 49, 50, 51, 53, 55, 57
Union Pacific Railroad, p. 13 (bottom), 16

Library of Congress Cataloging in Publication Data
ISBN 0-671-32871-9

Ditzel, Paul C
  Railroad yard.

    Includes index.
    SUMMARY: Describes the different types, functions,
and sizes of railroad yards and freight trains that pass
through them.
    1. Railroads—Yards—Juvenile literature.
[1. Railroads—Yards. 2. Railroads—Trains]
I. Title.
TF590.D57   625.1'8   77-12758
ISBN 0-671-32871-9

Acknowledgments

The Southern Pacific Transportation Company lived up to its motto, "The Friendly Southern Pacific" during the research, photography and writing of RAILROAD YARD. I am deeply grateful to Jim Shea, Vice President-Public Relations, to Tom Buckley, Los Angeles Manager of Public Relations for the railroad, and to Bill Robertson, Southern Pacific's legendary photographer. Together, they facilitated the solution of many problems associated with access and safety while photographing operations at the West Colton, California, railroad yard which has become a model for automated yards everywhere. Many SP officials and workers cooperated, too, and their patience in explaining the technicalities of this highly-computerized yard is much appreciated. Special mention must be made of the personal interest taken by Gary O'Malley, Yard Office Supervisor at West Colton. His profound loyalty to the Southern Pacific and to railroading in general did much to make my work easier. It was a great pleasure working with him, a feeling shared by Mike Meadows, my colleague whose photographic expertise is demonstrated in this book. I must also thank Hal Burroughs, Bill Cox and Gene Flohrschutz of the Santa Fe Railway's Los Angeles Public Relations staff and John Forbes and Al Krieg of the Union Pacific Railroad's Los Angeles Public Relations Department for their supplemental photographs and suggestions. My deep gratitude must also go to Ms. Anne O. Bennof, Manager, Educational and Informational Services, Association of American Railroads, Washington, D.C., for her advice and encouragement throughout this project. Last, but certainly far from least, I am profoundly appreciative of the many suggestions offered by my editor, Ms. Madelyn Anderson, whose deep interest in my book will not be forgotten by me.

Paul C. Ditzel
Northridge, California.

Books by Paul C. Ditzel
 RAILROAD YARD
 FIRE ENGINES, FIREFIGHTERS
 HOW THEY BUILT OUR NATIONAL MONUMENTS
 FIREFIGHTING: A New Look in The Old Firehouse
 EMERGENCY AMBULANCE
 FIRE ALARM! The Story of a Fire Department

DEDICATION

To Mrs. Marguerite Steiger and the late George C. Steiger, railroad friends from the halcyon days of the now all-but-forgotten Pere Marquette Railway.

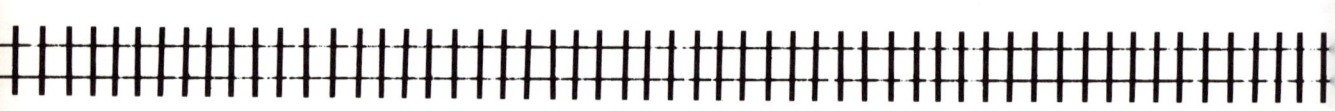

Contents

Introduction	9
The Yard	18
Receiving Yard	19
Cresting into the Bowl	26
Car Service Area	42
Diesel Service Area—the Roundhouse	47
Departure Yard	52
Glossary of Railroad Terms	60
Index	64

INTRODUCTION

Freight trains are a lot like relay runners—and railroad yards are the relay points. Starting at one yard, the train hurries to the next yard along its route. There it turns over its cars to another train being formed for still another yard, or to a local train for delivery to a nearby industry. A carload of freight often passes through many yards, each of them speedily relaying the car to its final destination.

The route of one boxcar was traced by a computer over a two-year period. The car started in a yard in St. Louis, Missouri. It crisscrossed the country in 70 different trains. It passed through 41

states, on the tracks and through the yards of 33 railroads, some of them many times. It carried loads ranging from paper to groceries. It traveled empty in only 14 trains—and those were trips to factories and warehouses for loading. A freight car does not stand idle for long. It must earn its keep by doing its job.

There are many sizes and types of yards. Some—usually those in smaller communities—handle only a few dozen cars a day. Others handle thousands. Among these larger yards are *gateway yards*, those in and around gateway cities. A gateway city is where tracks of one or more railroads end and those of other railroads begin.

Chicago, Illinois, is a gateway city—the nation's largest railroad center. Twenty-seven railroads connect at Chicago in more than two dozen yards.

Like Chicago, many gateways are in the middle part of the United States. The earliest railroads were built in the populated East. The Mississippi River, and towns along it, was our western frontier. When the movement westward grew, pushing our frontiers further west, railroads extended their tracks. And what was once western became mid-western. With the completion of the first transcontinental railroad in 1869, tracks were extended from Omaha, Nebraska, on the Missouri River, to California. This railroad, and others that followed it, played an important role in the settlement of the West. And today, more than 100 years later, Omaha is still a major railroad gateway city.

Completion of the first transcontinental railroad

In addition to gateway yards, there are special-purpose yards. Some are used to make up and service passenger trains. Some are yards that handle only one type of freight—coal, or ores, for example. *Unit trains*, or trains that carry only one kind of freight, such as coal, then go directly from yard to buyers, or to ports for shipment overseas. Coal companies are one of the railroads' largest customers.

Railroad yards have changed a lot from early days, when locomotives burned coal to make steam to power their engines. Then the coal smoke dirtied the air with soot, ash, carbon monoxide, and sulfur. Today's locomotives burn clean diesel oil, and are equipped with air and noise pollution control devices. The shrieking locomotive whistles and clanging bells are mostly gone. Noiseless signaling devices and noise-deadening barriers such as trees and shrubs help make today's yards quieter. Railroad yards try hard to be quiet neighbors so those people living around them can enjoy their homes while the railroads help to bring them the many things they need.

We use many products moved by train: frozen and canned foods, automobiles and parts, television sets, refrigerators, lumber, paper....

Serving the industries that make these things, the railroad yard sends out switching engines to pick up or deliver freight cars at *sidings*, tracks leading from the main line to factories and mills and other loading points.

For example, farmers bring their grain to storage elevators near a siding. The grain is loaded into covered *hopper cars* to be taken to a nearby yard. Here the cars will be formed into a train, along with cars from other sidings. The train will go to distant flour mills, where the grain will be unloaded through chutes that lead from doors at the bottom of the hopper car.

Thousands of trains a day carry many of the things we use in our daily lives. And special cars, like hopper cars, are used to carry them.

This airplane wing is going from factory to jet assembly plant in a specially built car.

Refrigerator cars keep foods from spoiling while they are being shipped. This refrigerator car is being loaded with tuna fish and catfood on a siding on the Los Angeles waterfront.

These Hy-Cubes, a little longer than a standard 79-foot bowling alley, were built to carry automobile parts.

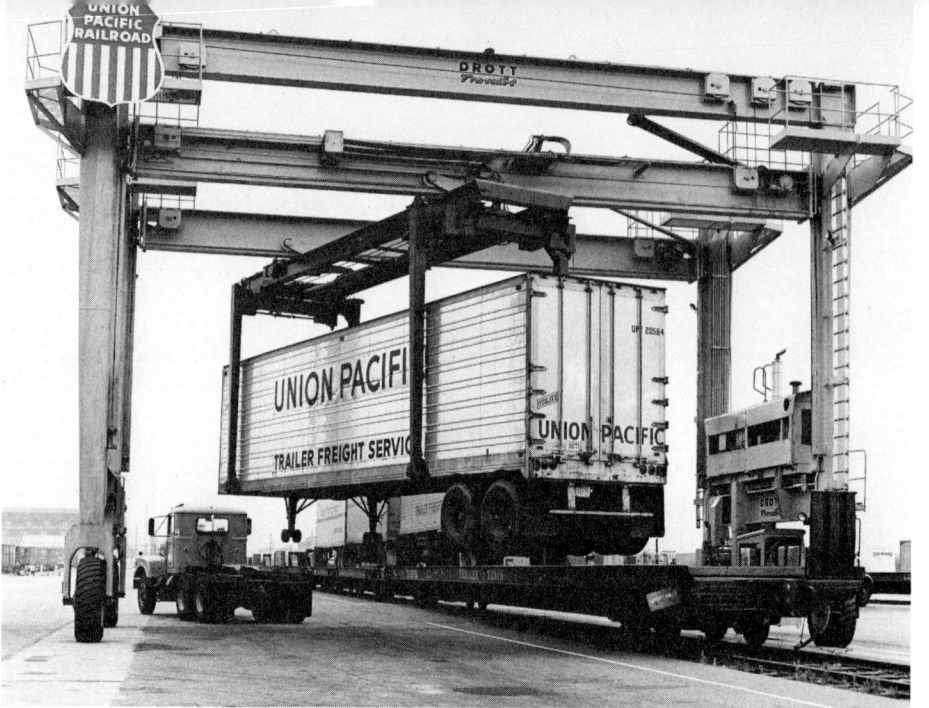

UNION PACIFIC RAILROAD
DROTT
UNION PACIFIC
TRAILER FREIGHT SERVIC
UNION PACIFIC

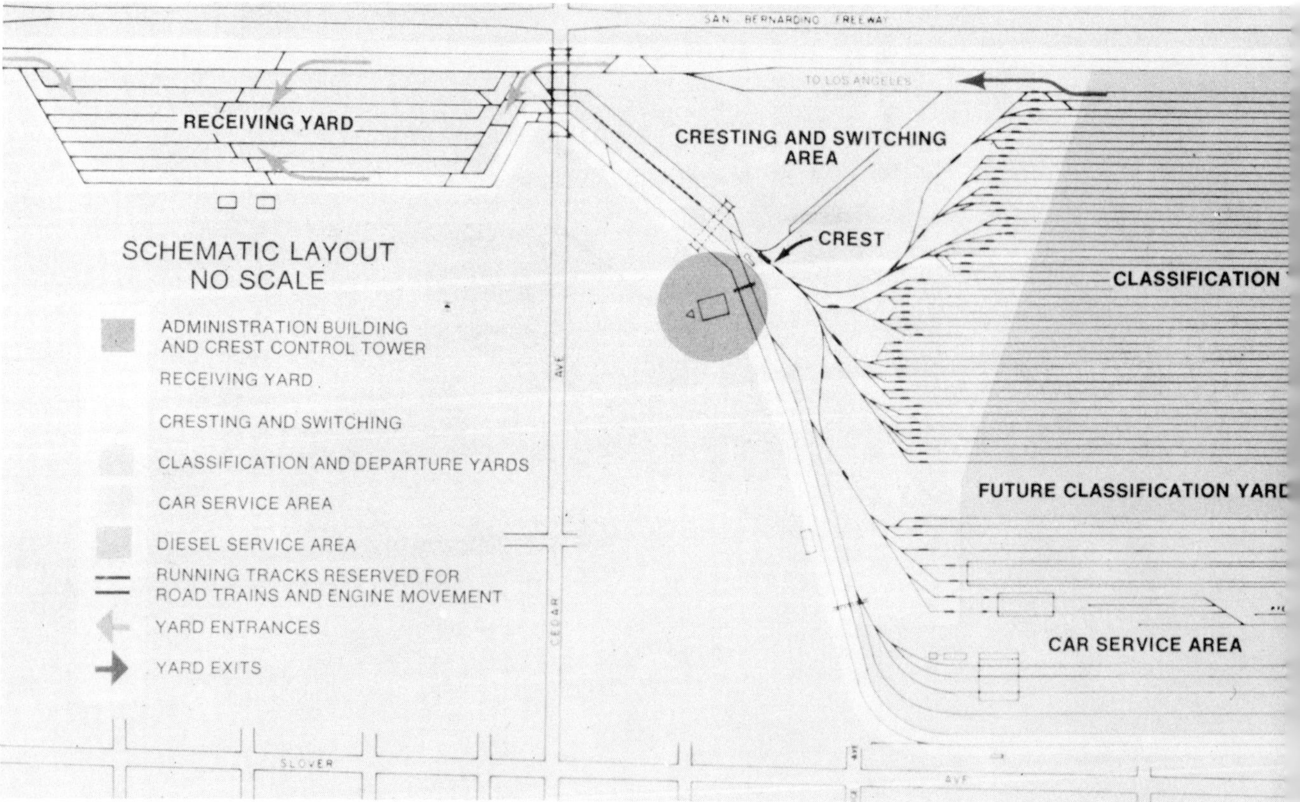
SAN BERNARDINO FREEWAY
TO LOS ANGELES
RECEIVING YARD
CRESTING AND SWITCHING AREA
CREST
CLASSIFICATION
SCHEMATIC LAYOUT
NO SCALE
ADMINISTRATION BUILDING AND CREST CONTROL TOWER
RECEIVING YARD
CRESTING AND SWITCHING
CLASSIFICATION AND DEPARTURE YARDS
CAR SERVICE AREA
DIESEL SERVICE AREA
RUNNING TRACKS RESERVED FOR ROAD TRAINS AND ENGINE MOVEMENT
YARD ENTRANCES
YARD EXITS
FUTURE CLASSIFICATION YARD
CAR SERVICE AREA
CEDAR
AVE
SLOVER
AVE

A truck trailer loaded with candy is lifted onto a flatcar. This is called a *piggyback*.

Piggyback and container trains travel faster than trucks. They also help rid the highways of traffic congestion.

Moving freight by rail also saves energy. Railroad locomotives can pull about four times more freight per gallon of fuel than big trucks, and 125 times more than airplanes.

To care for all these cars and the freight they carry, and to pass them along to their final destination, there are the railroad yards of the more than 365 railroads in the United States.

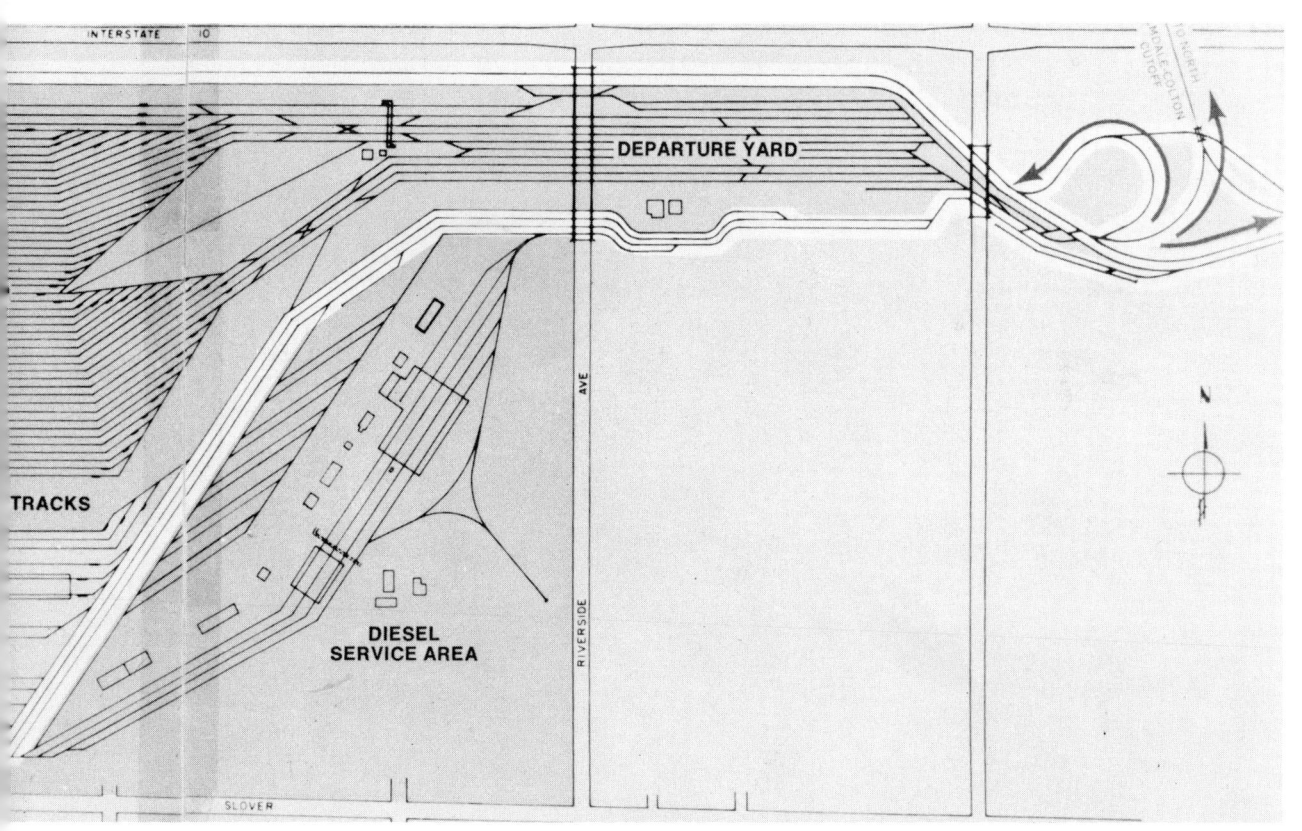

THE YARD

One of the newest and largest yards in the United States is the Southern Pacific's West Colton yard near Los Angeles.

The West Colton yard is six miles long. It contains 100 miles of track and 300 switches. *Switches* are the means by which locomotives and cars can be directed from one track into another.

Several thousand cars arrive here each day. They are sorted by destination into about 25 new trains going to other cities, and into local trains for delivery to nearby industrial sidings.

This is the story of how these thousands of cars are handled speedily, efficiently, and safely in the West Colton yard. It is also the story of what happens in railroad yards around the country.

Receiving Yard

Yardmaster Jerry Marble's office is high in the *control tower*, the nerve center of the railroad yard. Here is where all the traffic through the yard is controlled. And Jerry is in charge of the sorting process. He says, "Everything starts in the *receiving yard*, where all trains arrive from the main line."

After taking a sip of coffee from his "Big Daddy" mug, Jerry pushes buttons on his desk and asks a computer to show him the lineup of trains in the receiving yard. He also asks whether any other trains are due to arrive soon. The lineup in the receiving yard is instantly flashed on the television screen: about 1500 cars. And the computer says there's a 57-car train due in a few minutes from Los Angeles.

Let's watch it coming in and being processed through the yard.

At his desk, towerman Gary Baken opens switches and operates signals which will give the incoming train from Los Angeles a clear track into the receiving yard. Before him is a diagram of the switches and tracks in the receiving yard.

Rumbling past the signals and through one of the switches that Gary opened, the train from Los Angeles leaves the main line and enters the track leading into the receiving yard.

Soon after the train stops, the locomotives are *uncoupled*—separated—from the train. They are taken to the yard's diesel service area, where they will be made ready for their next trip.

The crew goes off duty until the crew dispatcher calls them to take out another train.

After the locomotives leave, Daniel Goode in the control tower gives the *blue-flag signal*. Blue lights flash on at each end of the track and light up the board in front of David. The train cannot be moved while it is blue-flagged, so yardmen can safely work around the cars. To railroaders everywhere, blue means safety.

Every car in the train is checked to make certain that brakes, wheels and other equipment are working properly so the car can safely continue its journey. Car Inspector Mariano Reyes said, "If I find anything that needs fixing, I'll B.O. it." Mariano explains that B.O. is railroad talk for Bad Order. A car that is Bad Ordered must be repaired before it can travel further.

Mariano sees a car with a broken fitting and B.O.'s it. It's a small job that a welder can fix in a few minutes. There's a welder and other repairmen riding in an electric-powered cart following Mariano. They make the repairs he marks on a tag attached to the car.

Now Mariano spots a broken ladder on a Milwaukee Road *gondola*, an open-top car. To fix it will require heavier equipment than the workmen carry in the cart. Using his walkie-talkie radio, Mariano calls the control tower and B.O.'s the car. A towerman punches the information into the computer so that the gondola will automatically be sent to the repair shop when it comes time to move the train.

Mariano also looks into all empty cars. If any need cleaning, he reports it to the tower. The computer is programmed to send these cars to the cleaning and upgrading area in the repair yard.

Special Agent Ernie Schueman also is looking over the train. Railroaders call these agents *Cinder Dicks*. Detectives are sometimes nicknamed "Dicks." And cinders from coal-burning locomotives were once used to build railroad yards. So—Cinder Dicks.

Ernie checks out an automobile carrier. "Look there," he says, "A broken window." Climbing up onto the car, Ernie finds a stone inside an automobile and makes out a report of the damage. The railroad will pay to fix it. "Luckily, nobody got hurt," says Ernie. "But not long ago, somebody threw a stone at a train and hit a brakeman in the head. He is paralyzed—will never walk again. We try hard to teach people through talks in schools and in newspaper articles that it is extremely dangerous to throw stones at trains."

Cinder Dicks also look for people who hitch rides on trains or those who have no business in the railroad yard. "It's not that we're mean," says Ernie, "but rather for their own safety. Many youngsters have lost arms or legs and have been killed while hitching rides or playing in railroad yards."

When the repairs are finished and the Cinder Dicks are done, the control tower is told that the blue-flag signals can be turned off. *Cresting*—sorting—can start.

Cresting Into the Bowl

In the control tower, Ernest Jones lines up switches to open a track leading from the receiving yard to the *cresting area*.

The crest is a low hill with a long down-hill slope on one side. It is called a *hump*. Switching locomotives push the cars up the hill. When they reach the top they are uncoupled and roll down the other side of the hill, onto a track in the *classification bowl*. This is called *cresting* or *humping*.

Railroads have used humps for cresting since the days of coal-burning locomotives. Cresting is the fastest, simplest and safest way to sort cars. Without humps, classifying or sorting would be a slow job because each car would have to be pushed or pulled by locomotives onto the proper classification bowl track.

Engineer Darrell Kendall gets the signal to bring his crest switching unit to the end of the train about to be crested. A crest switcher consists of two powerful diesel locomotives with a stubby unit—called a *slug*—coupled between them. The heavy slug has traction motors to give the locomotives a better grip on the track when they push the cars up the crest.

After coupling onto the end of the train, Darrell watches the speed indicator as he holds the brake lever. "The indicator says 0.0 right now," he says. "When the computer signals that it is okay to begin cresting, the speed indicator will automatically tell me how fast to safely push the cars up the crest. Usually it's about 4.5 miles an hour."

After getting the go-ahead signal, Darrell slowly pushes the throttle forward and the switching locomotives shove the train up the hill. The cars pass over a scale under the tracks. The scale weighs each car to find out if it is overloaded or whether the load inside has shifted. An unbalanced load is dangerous and could cause a wreck. If the car is overloaded or the load is unbalanced, the car will be crested onto a special track where corrective steps will be taken.

At the top of the crest is a signal box with five rows of lights, operated by the computer. They tell the waiting *pin-pullers* how many cars to uncouple. Here, the up-and-down row of lights on the left side of the box tell them that the first five cars are to go over the crest one at a time. Each car will be automatically switched to a different track in the classification bowl.

If a second white light flashed on next to any of the five, the pin-pullers would know the computer was telling them to uncouple two cars to go together to the same classification track.

The up-and-down row of lights on the right side are red. If, for any reason, cresting must suddenly stop, the red light flashes on, a warning horn blows—and all cresting is halted.

Pin-Pullers Walker Johnson and Kenneth Hayden reach between the first and second car and pull on long steel levers. For safety, the handles are located near the outer ends of the car. The levers release a *car-coupler* that is attached to both ends of every railroad car.

The cars uncouple. "Pop!" goes the air hose as the braking system automatically separates while the cars roll over the crest.

Again the computer in the control tower takes over. With lightning speed, it computes the weight of the car, how easily it rolls, and how far it must travel before it couples with other cars on the track picked out for it. Each track in the classification bowl usually holds cars for only one destination. But when the yard gets busy, several tracks may be chosen to hold all the cars going to a large gateway city.

Its track chosen, this carload of lumber picks up speed as it comes down from the crest. But waiting for it is the first of a series of *retarders* which slow the cars and keep them a safe distance apart.

"Poof!"—the air-operated retarders squeeze the wheels of the lumber car against the rails.

Rumbling further down the track, the lumber car heads for a second set of retarders which will slow its speed from 13 miles an hour to about nine. Still further on, a third set of retarders takes over to slow the car even more so that it will couple gently with the other cars on the track. Slow coupling speeds are important. They prevent cars from slamming together and damaging their cargo.

The next car down the crest is the Milwaukee Road gondola with the broken ladder that was B.O.'d in the Receiving Yard. The computer has not forgotten. It opens switches and directs the car along tracks leading to the repair area of the yard. There the ladder will be fixed.

Coming up the crest is a gigantic tank car. The warning horn honks, and a red light on the pin-pullers' signal box flashes on. All cresting stops.

"That's a 'K Car'," says Pin-Puller Hayden. "We give those babies special handling." He explains that a 'K Car' is the code name for cars containing hazardous materials. This tank car is loaded with a highly flammable liquefied gas. If the car somehow went off the tracks during cresting, the tank could split open and cause a disastrous explosion and fire. The danger of that happening is slight, but chance-taking is not part of safe railroading.

Engineer Kendall and his switching locomotives push the tank car onto a nearby track. In a little while, another switching unit will take the car to its proper place in the classification bowl.

The "K Car" safely out of the way, the horn blares an all-clear. Cresting starts again. Down the crest and across the retarders comes a boxcar that stands taller than most. It's fun to try to

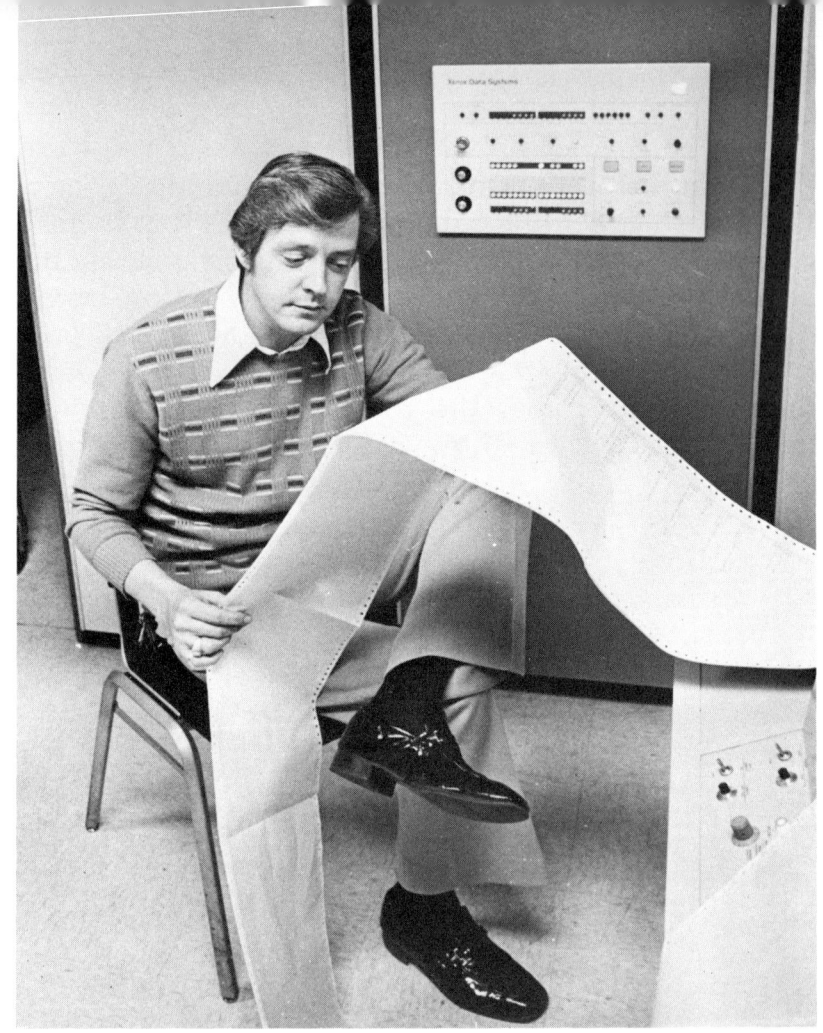

guess what's inside. Yard Office Supervisor Gary O'Malley can always check the computer printout for the answer. "Tall cars like that carry all kinds of bulky merchandise that can be stacked on top of each other," says Gary. "We used to call these extra tall ones 'Ugly Ducklings' because they stood out in a train of cars. But now they're common."

Guessing what might be inside the cars is fun, and so is seeing where the cars are from. Says Gary, "Any car in this yard that does not have Southern Pacific lettering is called a *foreign car*. That means the car belongs to another railroad. And every railroad has its own distinctive markings, called *heralds*. There are many of them."

There is a car from the Chessie System in the East. For years, the Chessie has used a kitten as part of its herald. The "C" in Chessie contains the outline of a kitten. The railroad says that freight traveling on the Chessie rides as contentedly as a sleeping kitten. "Purr-fect transportation," says the Chessie. "But then we think we have perfect transportation on the Southern Pacific, too," says Gary.

And here comes a car with a large circle with a white-dotted "i" inside it. "That's the herald of the Illinois Central Gulf Railroad," says Gary.

Even railroaders enjoy watching the cars. They look for drawings scrawled in chalk and crayon on the sides of cars. Who the artists are is a mystery. One of the more famous drawings is of a palm tree with a man wearing a sombrero sleeping under it. The drawing is signed "Herby." Who is Herby? Nobody in the yard is certain. But there is a story that Herby may be an East St. Louis, Illinois, worker who puts his mark on the side of every car he loads or unloads. There are said to be more than 400,000 Herby drawings riding the rails across the United States.

Another mysterious artist has marked hundreds of cars with a drawing of a bottle pouring champagne into a glass while bubbles rise from it. But the most famous freight car scribbler of them all was someone by the name of James B. King. He is believed to have started his artwork while he was working around Oregon and Washington. In flowing scrawl, he signed his name on the sides of cars and buildings. In time, railroaders recited a poem about him:

> Who is this fellow James B. King,
> Who writes his name on everything?
> James B. King on every wall,
> On flatcars low and boxcars tall,
> Whether he does it for money or fun,
> He sure is a scribbling son-of-a-gun!

Car Service Area

Cars needing major repairs are serviced in the *One-Spot shop*. It is called One-Spot because all heavy repairs can be done at this one location. Battery-operated trucks bring parts and equipment. Tools ranging from heavy sledge hammers to acetylene torches enable workers to quickly make repairs.

This One-Spot shop has 100-ton jacks which can lift an entire freight car so repairmen can

work underneath it. Welder Ben Fuentes begins work on the wheels that have been removed from the uplifted boxcar behind him. It takes only about 30 minutes to change wheels which have been worn flat by hard application of brakes.

The boxcar's wheels also need new brake shoes. Ben starts to put them on. There is one shoe for every wheel on a freight car. When the engineer applies air to the braking system of the train, the *brake shoes* automatically squeeze against the wheels to slow the train. Brake shoes are replaced when they wear down to a thickness of less than an inch. The new shoes are 1½-inches thick.

When Ben finishes his work, Carman Tony Madrid pushes a lever on a control panel. This turns on an underground cable which will bring the next car waiting in the service yard into the One-Spot.

The underground cable pulls a black-and-white striped iron bar that is called a *Rabbit*. The Rabbit travels out into the repair area, moves up against the wheel axle of the car to be fixed, and pushes it into the One-Spot.

After the cars are repaired, they are taken by a switching unit back to the cresting area and sent into the classification bowl.

Diesel Service Area -the Roundhouse

Locomotives are prepared in the yard's diesel service area for their next trip. Railroad workers call this area the roundhouse. But as you can see, it isn't round and it isn't a house. Many years ago, when the word was first used, it was. Steam locomotives could most easily be turned around for their next trip by putting them on a turntable. A roundhouse was built around the turntable and the locomotives were serviced there.

Because diesel locomotives can operate just as easily whichever way they are pointed, turntables are no longer needed. But the diesel service area kept its old name.

The diesel facility can service around 100 locomotives a day. Railroads often share their locomotives. If any one of these foreign locomotives needs repairs they will be done.

A shower bath is the first thing that happens to a locomotive when it comes to the roundhouse. Hot jets of water and detergents wash away the grime the locomotive has picked up during its long journey to the railroad yard. Then the locomotive is given a thorough rinsing.

The roundhouse has a water treatment system which recycles the rinse water so it can be used again. The system also separates oil from the water so that no oil enters the drains. The oil that is collected is also used again.

After its shower bath, the locomotive is driven onto a pad where it stands until it drips dry.

The locomotive is then taken to a service track for mechanical inspection and repairs. Locomotives are then lubricated and fueled with diesel oil.

Then the locomotives are filled with sand. Here, John Rodriguez uses a push-button device which sends sand shooting through his hose and into boxes in the locomotive. The engineers send streams of sand on the tracks to give their trains a better grip, or to help them stop.

Workers can make locomotives ready for another trip in as little as 2½ hours after they arrive in the yard. Diesels cost more than $400,000 apiece—too expensive to stand idle for long. And freight schedules must be met.

Work in the railroad yard goes on without stopping . . . night and day . . . every day of the year. Industries depend upon on-time delivery of freight. Assembly plants might be forced to close if parts are delayed. Customers would take business elsewhere. People would be out of work.

So, teamwork and speed are essential in the railroad yard.

Departure Yard

Now the cars are ready to be formed into trains. They are moved out of the classification bowl into the departure yard by a process called *trimming*.

There is a separate control tower for trimming. Here, Charles Cross gives the trim switching locomotive engineer the signal to begin building a train. This particular train will go to the north with cars for Los Angeles, Santa Barbara and San Luis Obispo, California.

Trains are built by joining together groups of cars called *blocks*. The block of cars that will be left at Los Angeles, the first stop, is put at the front of the train. The next stop is Santa Barbara. That block is put behind the Los Angeles block. The San Luis Obispo block is put at the end of the train.

As the blocks are joined, Switchman Frank Lawson guides the trim locomotive engineer to make sure the cars couple gently to prevent damage to the freight.

After the three blocks are coupled together, air brake hoses at the end of each car are connected to form a complete air line throughout the length of the train. In the trim control tower, Arthur Griffin pushes buttons which send air surging through the brake system. A light flashes on his desk-top display board—the brakes are working.

In the roundhouse, the locomotives are readied. Using a computer, the roundhouse foreman tells how many locomotives will be needed for each outbound train. A short train may need only one engine. But a long train with many loaded

cars that must climb a mountain may need five or more locomotives.

For this train, four locomotives are being used. They are being coupled to a train of 130 cars. The locomotives are controlled by the engineer, who rides behind the control throttle in the front locomotive. From here, he controls the speed of the train, watches the track ahead, and blares a horn warning at crossings. He is assisted by a fireman. This fireman has nothing to do with fires. His title is carried over from the days of steam-powered locomotives when the fireman shoveled coal into the firebox of the boiler.

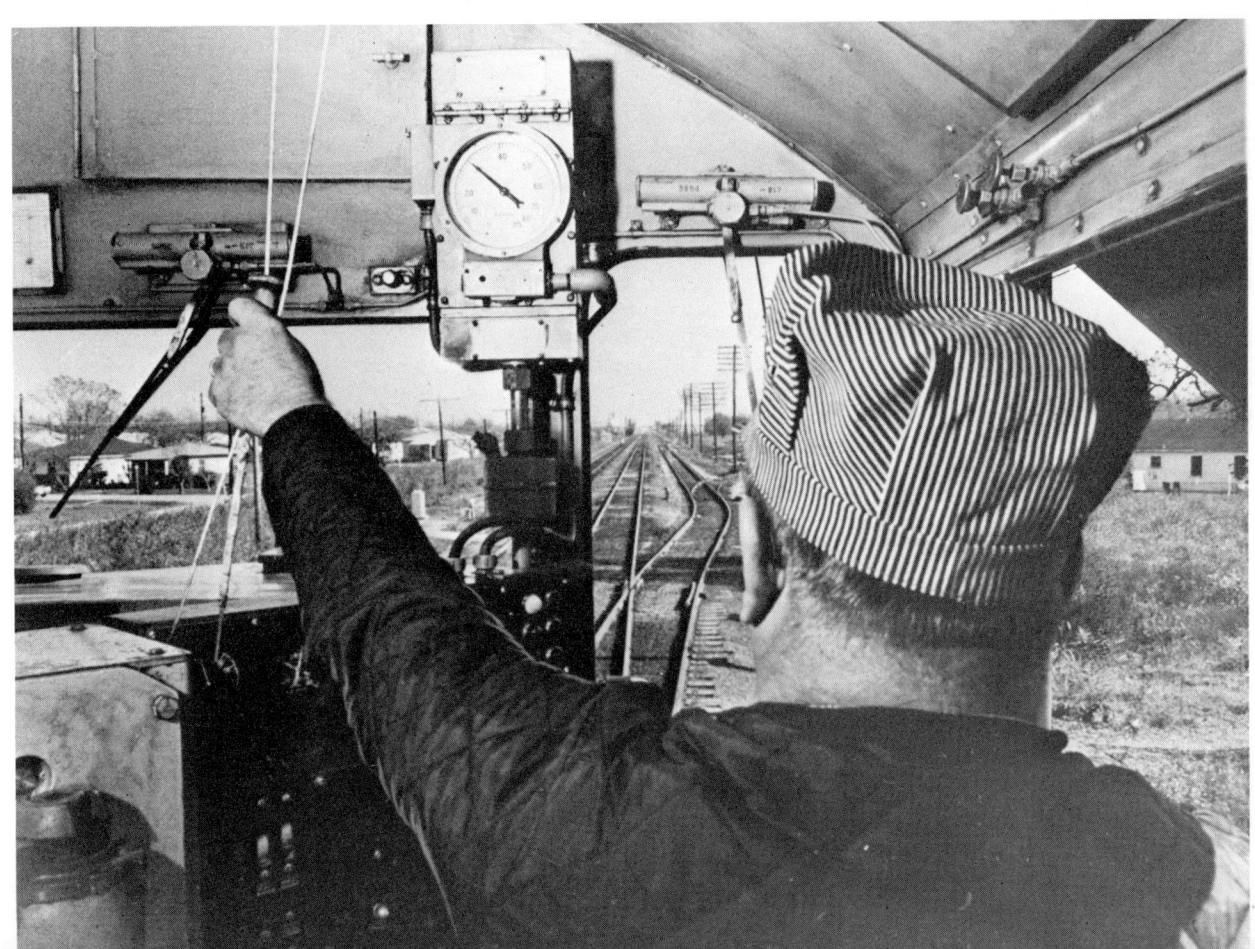

Now the caboose is coupled on. It has been brought in from the caboose servicing area outside the One-Spot. There the caboose was cleaned and supplied with ice water, towels and other necessities.

The caboose serves as an office for the conductor, who is in charge of the train. He does his paper work here, and he has a lot of it. Every car has a *waybill*, a sheet of paper showing what's in the car, who is shipping it, where it is going, and who will be receiving it.

Also in the caboose are the brakemen who keep watch on the train for any signs of mechanical trouble which would require the train to stop. At least one other brakeman rides up front. The crews in the caboose and in the locomotive keep in touch with one another by radio.

The train is completed now and crewmen are waiting for the signal to go. (Almost all freight crew members are men—but women are slowly starting to enter the field.)

The air brake hoses are connected and tested. Everything is okay. The train is mechanically safe to leave the yard.

The crew get their signal to go, and swing on board.

Switches are opened. A track entering the main line is cleared. Signals flash green. Slowly, the engineer pushes the throttle forward. Slowly, the four locomotives pull the train from the Departure Yard to the main line.

The end of the Departure Yard points east. But this train is going west, to Los Angeles. How does the train turn around? By means of a sweeping curve called a *balloon track*. The train looks like it is going in two directions at the same time —and it is! But not for long. Soon it reaches the main line and it heads for the next relay point— another railroad yard.

GLOSSARY of Railroad Terms

AIR MONKEY—Air brakes repairman.
ALLEY—A clear track.
BALLOON TRACK—A long, curved stretch of track that allows a train to turn to go in the opposite direction.
BEEHIVE—Yard office.
BEND THE IRON—To turn a track switch.
BIG OX—A train conductor.
BLOCK—A group of cars that will all be left at one station along the train's route.
BLUE-FLAG SIGNAL—The safety signal that keeps a train from moving, so that yardmen can work safely around the train.
B.O.—Bad Order. The marking of a car for repair.
BRAKE SHOE—A solid steel bar that rubs up against a railroad car wheel to stop the car from moving.
BRASS HAT—Any railroad official.
BROWNIES—Demerit marks placed against a worker's record for mistakes made.
BULL—See Cinder Dick.
CABOOSE—A railroad car for the train crew to ride or rest in. It is always the last car in a freight train.
CAR-COUPLING—The device on both ends of a railroad car that allows the automatic coupling of cars. *See also* Uncouple.
CAR-WHACKER—A car repairman.
COAL DRAG—A unit train made up of cars loaded only with coal. *See also* Unit Train.
CONTROL TOWER—An office containing equipment and signaling devices for controlling all traffic in the yard. It is located in a tower above the tracks of the yard.
CINDER CRUNCHER—A switchman.
CINDER DICK—A railroad policeman or yard detective.
CLASSIFICATION BOWL—A series of parallel tracks, all on a long slope so that railroad cars will coast downhill. *See also* Cresting Area; Hump.

CRESTING AREA—A low hill with a long downhill slope on one side, on which are the tracks of the Classification Bowl. *See also* Cresting.

CRESTING, or HUMPING—The process of pushing a train of cars slowly up one side of a cresting area hill, and letting them coast, one at a time, down the other side so that they can be switched on to the right trains being made up. See Trimming.

CRUMMY—A caboose.

CUPOLA—The dome in a caboose.

CUT—A group of cars that have been separated from the train as one unit. *See also* Block. There are usually from two to several cars in a cut or block.

DANCING ON A CARPET—Being called in to the superintendent's office, for investigation, complaints, or criticism.

DEPARTURE YARD—The area where Trimming takes place. See Trimming.

DIESEL SERVICE AREA—The part of the yard where locomotives are cleaned, repaired and refueled.

EAGLE EYE—Locomotive engineer.

FLOP—A bed.

FOREIGN CAR—A car that does not belong to the railroad that owns the yard.

GANDY DANCER—A track laborer who lays tracks or fixes rails and roadbed.

GARDEN—A railroad yard.

GATEWAY CITY—A city where the tracks of one or more railroads end and those of other railroads begin.

GATEWAY YARD—The railroad yard in a Gateway City.

GOAT—A yard engine.

GONDOLA—An open-top car, with low sides. It is also called a gon.

GO TO BEANS—Go eat.

GRAVEYARD WATCH—Working from 12:01 a.m. to 8 a.m.

HERALD—The markings on railroad cars that identify the railroad which owns the car.

HERDER—A railroad worker who couples engines on and takes them off on the arrival and departure of trains.

HIGHBALL—A signal that means full-speed ahead. It is made by swinging the hand or a lamp in a high wide arc.

HOG—A locomotive.
HOGGER—An engineer. Also called a Hoghead.
HOPPER CAR—An open-top railroad car with high sides, and with several compartments or "hoppers" inside, each with a door which opens from the bottom of the car. Hoppers carry only bulk cargo, such as coal, ore, sugar beets.
HOT SHOT—A fast train.
HUMP—A low hill. See Cresting; Cresting Area.
HUMPING—See Cresting.
HY-CUBE—A long car, specially built to carry automobile parts.
IN THE HOLE—A train on a siding, off the main line, to allow another train to pass it on the main line.
JAM BUSTER—Assistant yardmaster.
K-CAR—A railroad car that contains a dangerous cargo, and which must be handled separately and carefully.
KING—A freight train conductor; sometimes the yardmaster.
KNOWLEDGE BOX—The yardmaster's office.
LADDER—The main track of the freight yard system of tracks, from which all the other tracks lead off.
MASTER MANIAC—The master mechanic—an expert in repairs.
MUDHOP—A yard clerk.
NON-AIR—A non-union railroad worker.
OLD MAN—The superintendent.
ONE-SPOT SHOP—The place in the yard where all major repairs are made on railroad cars.
PIGGYBACK—The transporting of highway trailer trucks on specially built flatcars.
PIG PEN—Locomotive roundhouse.
PIN-PULLERS—The men who uncouple railroad cars.
RABBIT—A black and white striped iron bar attached to the end of an underground rope, and used to push cars into the One-Spot Shop.
RATTLER—A freight train.
RECEIVING YARD—The part of a railroad yard where trains enter to be crested and serviced.
RECYCLE—To make or reprocess for use again.
RED BALL—A fast freight train.
REEFER—A refrigerator car.

RETARDER—A device operated by air, used to slow cars down as they are coasting along down the slope of the Classification Bowl.

ROUNDHOUSE—The locomotive servicing area.

RULE G—The name railroaders use for the rule against drinking alcoholic beverages while on duty.

SIDING—Tracks that lead to factories or warehouses off the main line.

SLUG—A stubby locomotive unit coupled between two regular locomotives in a yard to help give better grip on the tracks when pushing cars up the hump for cresting.

SLAVE DRIVER—Yardmaster. *See also* Y.M.

SHINING TIME—Time to start work.

SUPERINTENDENT—Supervising official who is responsible to the yardmaster.

SWITCHES—The means by which trains are directed from one track to another.

TRAIN LINE—The pipe that carries air for the brakes through the total length of the train.

TRICK—A railroader's tour of duty.

TRIM CONTROL TOWER—A control tower for trimming. *See* Trimming.

TRIMMING—The process of joining together blocks of cars to form a train.

UNCOUPLE—To separate cars from each other.

UNIT TRAIN—A train made up of cars all carrying only one type of freight, and all going to the same place.

VARNISH—A passenger train.

WAYBILL—A document for each railroad car in a train. It shows what is in the car, who is shipping it, and who is receiving it.

WHEN DO YOU SHINE?—What time do you report for work?

Y.M.—Yardmaster.

Index

Air pollution, 12

B.O. (Bad Order), 23
Balloon track, 59
Blocks, blocking, 53
Blue-flag signal, 22
Boxcar, 9
Brake shoes, 44
Brakeman, 57

Caboose, 57
Car scribblers, 40, 41
Chicago, Ill., 10
Cinder Dicks, 24, 25
Conductor, 57
Control tower, 19
Coupling, 21, 31, 32
Cresting or humping, 26

Danger of throwing stones, playing in yards, 25, 26

East St. Louis, Ill., 40
Energy saving, 17
Engineer, 55

Fireman, 55
First transcontinental railroad, 10
Foreign car, 39

Gateway yards, 10, 11
Gondola car, 24

Heralds, 8, 39
Herby cartoons, 40
Hopper cars, 12
Humping. See Cresting

"K-Car," 36, 37

Los Angeles, Calif., 18, 52, 53, 59

Noise pollution, 12
Number of railroads in United States, 17

Omaha, Neb., 10

Piggyback car, 17
Pin-Pullers, 30, 31
Poem, 41

Rabbit, 46
Recycling oil, water, 48
Refrigerator car, 15
Retarders, 33, 35
Roundhouse, 47

St. Louis, Mo., 9
San Luis Obispo, Calif., 52, 53
Sand, 50
Santa Barbara, Calif., 52, 53
Sidings, 12
Slug, 28
Special purpose yards, 11
Switches, 18

Trimming, 52

"Ugly Ducklings," 38
Unit trains, 11

Waybill, 57
Weighing scale, 29
West Colton, Calif., 18
Women railroaders, 58